# Real Estate Field Notes

Find Your Next Property

REAL ESTATE FIELD NOTES

## Section 1

## Finding a Realtor

What am I looking for in a real estate agent?

# REAL ESTATE FIELD NOTES

Realtor #1

Realtor name
Phone
Email

☑ Verified Realtors License

How long have you been a real estate agent?

What is your personal style?

What do you look for in a property to help your buyers?

Do you have experience helping people purchase investment real estate?

Do you personally have your own investment real estate portfolio? If not, why? If so, how long have you been investing?

How many buyers are you currently representing? How many sellers are you currently representing? Is that lower than normal or higher than normal for you personally?

Will I be working with you? Or a member of your team? How big is your team?

Do you also offer property management services?

References

Reference #1
Name
Phone
Email
Best thing to say about the realtor
Worst thing to say about the realtor

Reference #2
Name
Phone
Email
Best thing to say about the realtor
Worst thing to say about the realtor

# REAL ESTATE FIELD NOTES

Realtor #2

Realtor name
Phone
Email

☑ Verified Realtors License

How long have you been a real estate agent?

What is your personal style?

What do you look for in a property to help your buyers?

Do you have experience helping people purchase investment real estate?

Do you personally have your own investment real estate portfolio? If not, why? If so, how long have you been investing?

How many buyers are you currently representing? How many sellers are you currently representing? Is that lower than normal or higher than normal for you personally?

Will I be working with you? Or a member of your team? How big is your team?

Do you also offer property management services?

References

Reference #1
Name
Phone
Email
Best thing to say about the realtor
Worst thing to say about the realtor

Reference #2
Name
Phone
Email
Best thing to say about the realtor
Worst thing to say about the realtor

# REAL ESTATE FIELD NOTES

Realtor #3

Realtor name
Phone
Email

☑ Verified Realtors License

How long have you been a real estate agent?

What is your personal style?

What do you look for in a property to help your buyers?

Do you have experience helping people purchase investment real estate?

Do you personally have your own investment real estate portfolio? If not, why? If so, how long have you been investing?

How many buyers are you currently representing? How many sellers are you currently representing? Is that lower than normal or higher than normal for you personally?

Will I be working with you? Or a member of your team? How big is your team?

Do you also offer property management services?

References

Reference #1
Name
Phone
Email
Best thing to say about the realtor
Worst thing to say about the realtor

Reference #2
Name
Phone
Email
Best thing to say about the realtor
Worst thing to say about the realtor

# REAL ESTATE FIELD NOTES

Realtor #4

Realtor name
Phone
Email

☑ Verified Realtors License

How long have you been a real estate agent?

What is your personal style?

What do you look for in a property to help your buyers?

Do you have experience helping people purchase investment real estate?

Do you personally have your own investment real estate portfolio? If not, why? If so, how long have you been investing?

How many buyers are you currently representing? How many sellers are you currently representing? Is that lower than normal or higher than normal for you personally?

Will I be working with you? Or a member of your team? How big is your team?

Do you also offer property management services?

References

Reference #1
Name
Phone
Email
Best thing to say about the realtor
Worst thing to say about the realtor

Reference #2
Name
Phone
Email
Best thing to say about the realtor
Worst thing to say about the realtor

# REAL ESTATE FIELD NOTES

Realtor #5

Realtor name
Phone
Email

☑ Verified Realtors License

How long have you been a real estate agent?

What is your personal style?

What do you look for in a property to help your buyers?

Do you have experience helping people purchase investment real estate?

Do you personally have your own investment real estate portfolio? If not, why? If so, how long have you been investing?

How many buyers are you currently representing? How many sellers are you currently representing? Is that lower than normal or higher than normal for you personally?

Will I be working with you? Or a member of your team? How big is your team?

Do you also offer property management services?

References

Reference #1
Name
Phone
Email
Best thing to say about the realtor
Worst thing to say about the realtor

Reference #2
Name
Phone
Email
Best thing to say about the realtor
Worst thing to say about the realtor

REAL ESTATE FIELD NOTES

Realtor #6

Realtor name
Phone
Email

☑ Verified Realtors License

How long have you been a real estate agent?

What is your personal style?

What do you look for in a property to help your buyers?

Do you have experience helping people purchase investment real estate?

Do you personally have your own investment real estate portfolio? If not, why? If so, how long have you been investing?

How many buyers are you currently representing? How many sellers are you currently representing? Is that lower than normal or higher than normal for you personally?

Will I be working with you? Or a member of your team? How big is your team?

Do you also offer property management services?

References

Reference #1
Name
Phone
Email
Best thing to say about the realtor
Worst thing to say about the realtor

Reference #2
Name
Phone
Email
Best thing to say about the realtor
Worst thing to say about the realtor

# REAL ESTATE FIELD NOTES

Realtor #7

Realtor name
Phone
Email

☑ Verified Realtors License

How long have you been a real estate agent?

What is your personal style?

What do you look for in a property to help your buyers?

Do you have experience helping people purchase investment real estate?

Do you personally have your own investment real estate portfolio? If not, why? If so, how long have you been investing?

How many buyers are you currently representing? How many sellers are you currently representing? Is that lower than normal or higher than normal for you personally?

Will I be working with you? Or a member of your team? How big is your team?

Do you also offer property management services?

References

Reference #1
Name
Phone
Email
Best thing to say about the realtor
Worst thing to say about the realtor

Reference #2
Name
Phone
Email
Best thing to say about the realtor
Worst thing to say about the realtor

# REAL ESTATE FIELD NOTES

Realtor #8

Realtor name
Phone
Email

☑ Verified Realtors License

How long have you been a real estate agent?

What is your personal style?

What do you look for in a property to help your buyers?

Do you have experience helping people purchase investment real estate?

Do you personally have your own investment real estate portfolio? If not, why? If so, how long have you been investing?

How many buyers are you currently representing? How many sellers are you currently representing? Is that lower than normal or higher than normal for you personally?

Will I be working with you? Or a member of your team? How big is your team?

Do you also offer property management services?

References

Reference #1
Name
Phone
Email
Best thing to say about the realtor
Worst thing to say about the realtor

Reference #2
Name
Phone
Email
Best thing to say about the realtor
Worst thing to say about the realtor

# REAL ESTATE FIELD NOTES

Realtor #9

Realtor name
Phone
Email

☑ Verified Realtors License

How long have you been a real estate agent?

What is your personal style?

What do you look for in a property to help your buyers?

Do you have experience helping people purchase investment real estate?

Do you personally have your own investment real estate portfolio? If not, why? If so, how long have you been investing?

How many buyers are you currently representing? How many sellers are you currently representing? Is that lower than normal or higher than normal for you personally?

Will I be working with you? Or a member of your team? How big is your team?

Do you also offer property management services?

References

Reference #1
Name
Phone
Email
Best thing to say about the realtor
Worst thing to say about the realtor

Reference #2
Name
Phone
Email
Best thing to say about the realtor
Worst thing to say about the realtor

# REAL ESTATE FIELD NOTES

Realtor #10

Realtor name
Phone
Email

☑ Verified Realtors License

How long have you been a real estate agent?

What is your personal style?

What do you look for in a property to help your buyers?

Do you have experience helping people purchase investment real estate?

Do you personally have your own investment real estate portfolio? If not, why? If so, how long have you been investing?

How many buyers are you currently representing? How many sellers are you currently representing? Is that lower than normal or higher than normal for you personally?

Will I be working with you? Or a member of your team? How big is your team?

Do you also offer property management services?

References

Reference #1
Name
Phone
Email
Best thing to say about the realtor
Worst thing to say about the realtor

Reference #2
Name
Phone
Email
Best thing to say about the realtor
Worst thing to say about the realtor

# REAL ESTATE FIELD NOTES

Top 2 or 3 agents

What do I like about each of them? Which direction am I leaning?

Final decision

REAL ESTATE FIELD NOTES

# Section 2

# Finding a Property

Global questions: how much cash do I have?

How much loan have I been approved for?

What area am I searching in?

What am I looking for?

Why do I want a property in this area?

Is now a good time to buy? Why?

How many units?

Total size of the property. Size of each unit.

# REAL ESTATE FIELD NOTES

Property #1

Why are you selling?

How long has the house been on the market?

How much did the seller pay for the home?

Has the seller dropped the price already? If so, what was the original asking price?

What's wrong with it? List ALL repairs needed and cost.

What have been some of the past problems that have already been fixed. (they do not need to be disclosed, but there's a chance that I may come up again)

How old is the roof?
Water heater?
Furnace?
Air conditioning?

Are the bathrooms renovated?

Is the kitchen renovated?

Do all renovations have a permit?


If a rental property, are there currently tenants? If so, what's their monthly rent? How long remaining in the lease? Have there been lease increases over the lifetime of the tenancy? Any complaints from the tenants?


Subjective assessment
What do I personally like or dislike about the property? Gut feelings? Can I see myself owning this property? Does it fit into my total life?


What does me wife/husband think about the property?

# REAL ESTATE FIELD NOTES

Property #2

Why are you selling?

How long has the house been on the market?

How much did the seller pay for the home?

Has the seller dropped the price already? If so, what was the original asking price?

What's wrong with it? List ALL repairs needed and cost.

What have been some of the past problems that have already been fixed. (they do not need to be disclosed, but there's a chance that I may come up again)

How old is the roof?
Water heater?
Furnace?
Air conditioning?

Are the bathrooms renovated?

Is the kitchen renovated?

Do all renovations have a permit?


If a rental property, are there currently tenants? If so, what's their monthly rent? How long remaining in the lease? Have there been lease increases over the lifetime of the tenancy? Any complaints from the tenants?


Subjective assessment
What do I personally like or dislike about the property? Gut feelings? Can I see myself owning this property? Does it fit into my total life?


What does me wife/husband think about the property?

# REAL ESTATE FIELD NOTES

Property #3

Why are you selling?

How long has the house been on the market?

How much did the seller pay for the home?

Has the seller dropped the price already? If so, what was the original asking price?

What's wrong with it? List ALL repairs needed and cost.

What have been some of the past problems that have already been fixed. (they do not need to be disclosed, but there's a chance that I may come up again)

How old is the roof?
Water heater?
Furnace?
Air conditioning?

Are the bathrooms renovated?

Is the kitchen renovated?

Do all renovations have a permit?


If a rental property, are there currently tenants? If so, what's their monthly rent? How long remaining in the lease? Have there been lease increases over the lifetime of the tenancy? Any complaints from the tenants?


Subjective assessment
What do I personally like or dislike about the property? Gut feelings? Can I see myself owning this property? Does it fit into my total life?


What does me wife/husband think about the property?

# REAL ESTATE FIELD NOTES

Property #3

Why are you selling?

How long has the house been on the market?

How much did the seller pay for the home?

Has the seller dropped the price already? If so, what was the original asking price?

What's wrong with it? List ALL repairs needed and cost.

What have been some of the past problems that have already been fixed. (they do not need to be disclosed, but there's a chance that I may come up again)

How old is the roof?
Water heater?
Furnace?
Air conditioning?

Are the bathrooms renovated?

Is the kitchen renovated?

Do all renovations have a permit?


If a rental property, are there currently tenants? If so, what's their monthly rent? How long remaining in the lease? Have there been lease increases over the lifetime of the tenancy? Any complaints from the tenants?


Subjective assessment
What do I personally like or dislike about the property? Gut feelings? Can I see myself owning this property? Does it fit into my total life?


What does me wife/husband think about the property?

# REAL ESTATE FIELD NOTES

Property #4

Why are you selling?

How long has the house been on the market?

How much did the seller pay for the home?

Has the seller dropped the price already? If so, what was the original asking price?

What's wrong with it? List ALL repairs needed and cost.

What have been some of the past problems that have already been fixed. (they do not need to be disclosed, but there's a chance that I may come up again)

How old is the roof?
Water heater?
Furnace?
Air conditioning?

Are the bathrooms renovated?

Is the kitchen renovated?

Do all renovations have a permit?


If a rental property, are there currently tenants? If so, what's their monthly rent? How long remaining in the lease? Have there been lease increases over the lifetime of the tenancy? Any complaints from the tenants?


Subjective assessment
What do I personally like or dislike about the property? Gut feelings? Can I see myself owning this property? Does it fit into my total life?


What does me wife/husband think about the property?

# REAL ESTATE FIELD NOTES

Property #5

Why are you selling?

How long has the house been on the market?

How much did the seller pay for the home?

Has the seller dropped the price already? If so, what was the original asking price?

What's wrong with it? List ALL repairs needed and cost.

What have been some of the past problems that have already been fixed. (they do not need to be disclosed, but there's a chance that I may come up again)

How old is the roof?
Water heater?
Furnace?
Air conditioning?

Are the bathrooms renovated?

Is the kitchen renovated?

Do all renovations have a permit?


If a rental property, are there currently tenants? If so, what's their monthly rent? How long remaining in the lease? Have there been lease increases over the lifetime of the tenancy? Any complaints from the tenants?


Subjective assessment
What do I personally like or dislike about the property? Gut feelings? Can I see myself owning this property? Does it fit into my total life?


What does me wife/husband think about the property?

# REAL ESTATE FIELD NOTES

Property #6

Why are you selling?

How long has the house been on the market?

How much did the seller pay for the home?

Has the seller dropped the price already? If so, what was the original asking price?

What's wrong with it? List ALL repairs needed and cost.

What have been some of the past problems that have already been fixed. (they do not need to be disclosed, but there's a chance that I may come up again)

How old is the roof?
Water heater?
Furnace?
Air conditioning?

Are the bathrooms renovated?

Is the kitchen renovated?

Do all renovations have a permit?


If a rental property, are there currently tenants? If so, what's their monthly rent? How long remaining in the lease? Have there been lease increases over the lifetime of the tenancy? Any complaints from the tenants?


Subjective assessment
What do I personally like or dislike about the property? Gut feelings? Can I see myself owning this property? Does it fit into my total life?


What does me wife/husband think about the property?

# REAL ESTATE FIELD NOTES

Property #7

Why are you selling?

How long has the house been on the market?

How much did the seller pay for the home?

Has the seller dropped the price already? If so, what was the original asking price?

What's wrong with it? List ALL repairs needed and cost.

What have been some of the past problems that have already been fixed. (they do not need to be disclosed, but there's a chance that I may come up again)

How old is the roof?
Water heater?
Furnace?
Air conditioning?

Are the bathrooms renovated?

Is the kitchen renovated?

Do all renovations have a permit?


If a rental property, are there currently tenants? If so, what's their monthly rent? How long remaining in the lease? Have there been lease increases over the lifetime of the tenancy? Any complaints from the tenants?


Subjective assessment
What do I personally like or dislike about the property? Gut feelings? Can I see myself owning this property? Does it fit into my total life?


What does me wife/husband think about the property?

# REAL ESTATE FIELD NOTES

Property #8

Why are you selling?

How long has the house been on the market?

How much did the seller pay for the home?

Has the seller dropped the price already? If so, what was the original asking price?

What's wrong with it? List ALL repairs needed and cost.

What have been some of the past problems that have already been fixed. (they do not need to be disclosed, but there's a chance that I may come up again)

How old is the roof?
Water heater?
Furnace?
Air conditioning?

Are the bathrooms renovated?

Is the kitchen renovated?

Do all renovations have a permit?


If a rental property, are there currently tenants? If so, what's their monthly rent? How long remaining in the lease? Have there been lease increases over the lifetime of the tenancy? Any complaints from the tenants?


Subjective assessment
What do I personally like or dislike about the property? Gut feelings? Can I see myself owning this property? Does it fit into my total life?


What does me wife/husband think about the property?

# REAL ESTATE FIELD NOTES

Property #9

Why are you selling?

How long has the house been on the market?

How much did the seller pay for the home?

Has the seller dropped the price already? If so, what was the original asking price?

What's wrong with it? List ALL repairs needed and cost.

What have been some of the past problems that have already been fixed. (they do not need to be disclosed, but there's a chance that I may come up again)

How old is the roof?
Water heater?
Furnace?
Air conditioning?

Are the bathrooms renovated?

Is the kitchen renovated?

Do all renovations have a permit?


If a rental property, are there currently tenants? If so, what's their monthly rent? How long remaining in the lease? Have there been lease increases over the lifetime of the tenancy? Any complaints from the tenants?


Subjective assessment
What do I personally like or dislike about the property? Gut feelings? Can I see myself owning this property? Does it fit into my total life?


What does me wife/husband think about the property?

# REAL ESTATE FIELD NOTES

Property #10

Why are you selling?

How long has the house been on the market?

How much did the seller pay for the home?

Has the seller dropped the price already? If so, what was the original asking price?

What's wrong with it? List ALL repairs needed and cost.

What have been some of the past problems that have already been fixed. (they do not need to be disclosed, but there's a chance that I may come up again)

How old is the roof?
Water heater?
Furnace?
Air conditioning?

Are the bathrooms renovated?

Is the kitchen renovated?

Do all renovations have a permit?


If a rental property, are there currently tenants? If so, what's their monthly rent? How long remaining in the lease? Have there been lease increases over the lifetime of the tenancy? Any complaints from the tenants?


Subjective assessment
What do I personally like or dislike about the property? Gut feelings? Can I see myself owning this property? Does it fit into my total life?


What does me wife/husband think about the property?

# REAL ESTATE FIELD NOTES

Side-by-side analysis.

Which properties am I going to make an offer? How much will I offer, and why?

Counter offers

Do I still want to go through with it? How bad do I want it?

Accepted offer?

# REAL ESTATE FIELD NOTES

NOTES

# REAL ESTATE FIELD NOTES

NOTES

# REAL ESTATE FIELD NOTES

NOTES

REAL ESTATE FIELD NOTES

NOTES

# REAL ESTATE FIELD NOTES

NOTES

www.ingramcontent.com/pod-product-compliance
Lightning Source LLC
Chambersburg PA
CBHW081709220526
45466CB00009B/2933